GROUNDHOG WEATHER SCHOOL

illustrated by

JOAN HOLUB · KRISTIN SORRA

SCHOLASTIC INC.
New York Toronto London Auckland
Sydney Mexico City New Delhi Hong Kong

ISBN 978-0-545-33177-7

12 11 10 9 8 7 6 5 4   12 13 14 15 16/0

Printed in the U.S.A.   40

First Scholastic printing, January 2011

Design by Katrina Damkoehler
Text set in Burghley Medium
The artist used hand-painted textures of oil on paper, found objects and papers,
all combined and rendered in Photoshop to create the illustrations for this book.

For Kristen Shaheen and Paul Holub—J.H.

For David, Marlene & Noah—K.S.

The little store
FOR YOUR HIBERNATION NEE...

72 BURROW STREET

HAVE YOU GOT WHAT IT TAKES TO BE A WEATHER FORECASTER?

Take this quiz and check all that apply:

Prof. W. Groundhog

☐ **ARE YOU A MAMMAL?**
(If you are warm-blooded, have a backbone, and drank milk as a baby, you probably are.)

☐ **ARE YOU FURRY?**
(You be the judge.)

☐ **DO YOU LIVE IN A BURROW?**
(If you live in a hole or a tunnel dug in the ground, check this box.)

☐ **ARE YOU A RODENT?**
(If you have 2 front teeth that never stop growing, you probably are.)

☐ **ARE YOU AN HERBIVORE?**
(If you only eat plants, you are.)

☐ **DO YOU HIBERNATE?**
(If you sleep for months at a time each winter, you're a hibernator all righty.)

If you checked all 6 boxes, you're invited to attend GROUNDHOG WEATHER SCHOOL!

Burbank's
RESTAURANT
PIG

Welcome to your first day at Groundhog Weather School, class. Let's begin by saying the pledge.

PLEDGE of HOG-ALLEGIANCE

We, the students of
Groundhog Weather School,
pledge to come out of our burrows
on February second
to look for our shadows,
and to remember that
if we don't see our shadows,
it means spring is here;
if we do see our shadows,
it means there'll be
six more weeks of winter.

FOX

DOG

WOLF

BOBCAT

HAWK

OWL

EAGLE

HUMAN

Most of us live in areas that get very cold in winter, like the northeast or central part of the United States and in Canada.

Groundhog Day began here in Pennsylvania.

We dig holes and eat farm crops. So some states don't allow groundhogs— except for graduates of Groundhog Weather School, of course!

Like most groundhogs in the northeastern United States, I prefer to be called a woodchuck. In the Appalachian Mountains, groundhogs are called whistle pigs because we whistle to warn other groundhogs of danger.

RANGE OF GROUNDHOGS IN NORTH AMERICA

Well done, class! Now let's visit the library. Research reports are due on the next page.

FAMOUS ★ FURRY ★ HOGNOSTICATORS

Punxsutawney Phil
Punxsutawney, Pennsylvania
• made his first weather prediction in 1886
• met U.S. President Ronald Reagan
• starred in a movie called Groundhog Day

Wiarton Willie
Wiarton, Ontario, Canada
• a rare white (albino) groundhog with pink eyes
• tries to predict which football team will win the Super Bowl
• gets visitors from as far away as Pakistan

General Beauregard Lee
Lilburn, Georgia
• lives in a small white house at the Yellow River Game Ranch
• has been on the Today show and on Animal Planet
• has an honorary college degree

Jimmy the Groundhog
Sun Prairie, Wisconsin

• is visited by as many as 500 people each Groundhog Day
• has a weather hotline
• visits Wisconsin schools

Buckeye Chuck
Marion, Ohio

• the official Ohio state
groundhog
• lives in a comfy
straw-lined box in a park
• visits a radio station on
Groundhog Day to give his
weather forecast

Pierre C. Shadeaux
New Iberia, Louisiana
• is really a nutria, a
rodent with webbed feet
and a long tail that lives
in marshland or swamps
• has a Cajun-style house,
which is moved to the
Bouligny Plaza park each
year for a big Groundhog
Day celebration

Staten Island Chuck
Staten Island, New York
• has a house with a
thermometer in the roof
• lives at the Staten Island Zoo
• ice statues of him are carved
on February 2

Sir Walter Wally
Raleigh, North Carolina

• in the week before Groundhog Day, kids record their
weather observations. When
the mayor announces Wally's
weather forecast at the North
Carolina Museum of Natural
Sciences, kids watch to see
if Wally's prediction turns
out to be right

NATURE'S WEATHER PREDICTORS

Some plants and animals can help predict the weather.

A tree's leaves can predict storms. Leaves curl upward so their underside shows if there is moisture in the air and a strong wind is blowing.

ACHOO!

Cows don't like wind blowing in their faces, so they stand with their backsides to the wind. Winds blowing from the west usually bring good weather. So if a cow's tail is turned toward the west, it often means good weather is coming.

Wet honeybees are too heavy to fly. They stay near their hive if rain is coming.

If a pinecone's leaves fold inward, it may rain. In dry weather, they fold outward.

Moo!

Moo to you too.

LUKE HOWARD created a system for classifying and naming different cloud shapes. It includes cumulus, cirrus, and stratus clouds.

WILSON "SNOWFLAKE" BENTLEY was a farmer in Vermont who took thousands of pictures of individual snowflakes. This helped scientists understand how snowflakes form.

WEATHER MEN

BAROMETER

Impressive.

EVANGELISTA TORRICELLI invented the barometer, which measures air pressure. If air is not pressing hard against the earth, it's called a low-pressure system. That often means it will rain. Can you guess what a high-pressure system means?

PROFESSOR THEODORE FUJITA was nicknamed "Mr. Tornado" because he helped figure out how to measure the wind speed inside a tornado.

Lunchtime, everyone! Be sure you hog out. It's important to add as much fat to our bodies as we can before hibernation begins.

Why do we have to hibernate in the winter?

Yeah! I'm not sleepy.

We hibernate for four or five months between October and March because it's cold and food is hard to find.

During hibernation we are in a deep sleep. Our heartbeats slow down, our body temperatures drop, and we only breathe about once every four minutes! We don't need to eat because we live off of the fat our bodies have stored. So eat up, groundhogs!

My friend Frog hibernates at the bottom of a stream where the water doesn't freeze.

My friend Bat hibernates in a cave, with her wings tucked close to keep her warm.

HOW TO BUILD A BURROW

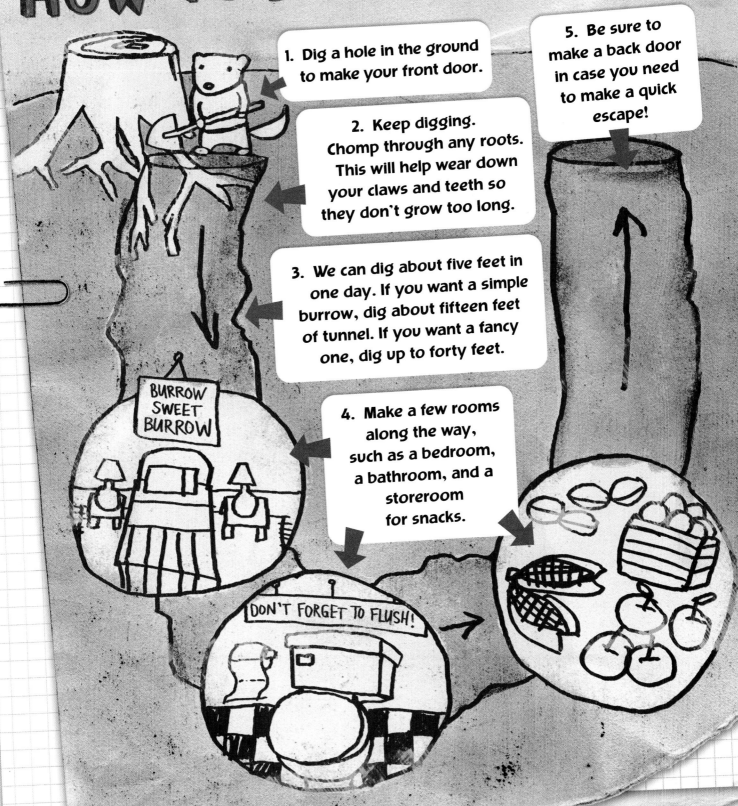

1. Dig a hole in the ground to make your front door.

2. Keep digging. Chomp through any roots. This will help wear down your claws and teeth so they don't grow too long.

3. We can dig about five feet in one day. If you want a simple burrow, dig about fifteen feet of tunnel. If you want a fancy one, dig up to forty feet.

4. Make a few rooms along the way, such as a bedroom, a bathroom, and a storeroom for snacks.

5. Be sure to make a back door in case you need to make a quick escape!

BURROW SWEET BURROW

DON'T FORGET TO FLUSH!

There are two reasons why we have seasons:
1. Planet Earth orbits (goes around) the sun.
2. The Earth is tilted.

The equator is an imaginary line that divides Earth into two halves called hemispheres. When a hemisphere tilts toward the sun, it's warmer, as in summer. When it tilts away, it's colder, as in winter.

I'm fall. I begin around September 21 at the fall equinox, when day and night are the same length.

Wonderful. I'm so proud of you!

the BIG test

A MULTIPLE CHOICE QUIZ

Please circle the correct answer:

1. What day do you come out of your burrow?
   a. on your birthday
   b. on February 2nd
   c. on February 32nd

2. What do you look for when you come out?
   a. a valentine
   b. a shadow
   c. a pot of gold

3. If you see it (see answer to number 2), what does it mean?
   a. spring is here
   b. summer vacation is here
   c. six more weeks of winter

4. If you don't see it, what does it mean?
   a. you are invisible
   b. spring is here
   c. six more years of school

5. Whether you see it or not, what's the next thing you do?
   a. go back to sleep
   b. have a snack
   c. report the results to Groundhog Headquarters

(Answers: 1b, 2b, 3c, 4b, 5c)

That's one BIG test!

OCTOBER
Columbus Day

Texas

New York

Florida

California

NOVEMBER
Thanksgiving

DECEMBER
Christmas, Hanukkah

JANUARY
Martin Luther King Jr. Day

FEB 2nd...
Wake up! IT'S GROUNDHOG DAY!

How did Groundhog Day get started?

Long ago, farmers in Europe watched for badgers and bears to wake up from hibernation, hoping this indicated that winter had ended. If spring was coming, it would be safe to plant crops without worrying they might freeze. When these farmers settled in Pennsylvania in the 1700s, there were lots of groundhogs around, so the farmers began watching them wake up instead.

But why choose February 2?

Ancient Romans and other past civilizations could hardly wait for warm spring weather to arrive. February 2 comes about halfway between the shortest day of the year (December 21) and the beginning of spring (March 21), so it was a good day to celebrate the coming season. In North America, these February 2 celebrations became Groundhog Day.

Who's better at predicting the weather—a groundhog or you?

Groundhog weather predictions are only right about one third of the time. But it's fun to celebrate Groundhog Day and watch for winter to eventually turn into spring. This February 2, do you hope spring will come right away or do you hope winter lasts longer? Which do you think will happen? Write down your prediction and see if it comes true.

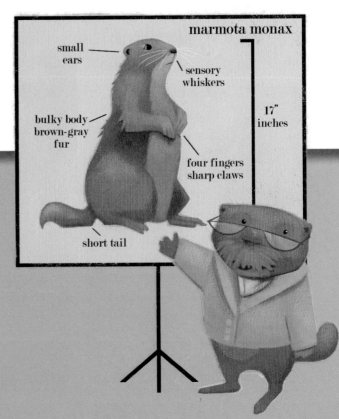

marmota monax

small ears

sensory whiskers

17" inches

bulky body brown-gray fur

four fingers sharp claws

short tail